DATE DUE

	NOV 2 4 2010		
	WITHDRAWN		

JUL 1 5 2000

Swoon Noir

swoon noir

BRUCE ANDREWS

chax press 2007

Printed in the United States of America

Published by
Chax Press
101 W. Sixth Street
Tucson, Arizona 85701-1000

ISBN 978-0-925904-48-5

For the first appearances of some of these texts, great thanks to the editors &
publishers of: *American Letters & Commentary, Angelaki, Big Allis, BOO, Bullhead,
Capilano Review, Combo, Fence, House Organ, Lungfull, Object, Rhizome, Ribot,
Talisman, Tight, Torque, West Coast Line.*

contents

finite until

Only the easy is

vicarious pirating the tumble blab on

fear critiques allocative trance rep mother slung over

subject-matter mass adheres mummy mutant

preranked vetting night-quickened leisure dolls

Hosing down the intervals, exult stunts

smoother wobbling saboteurs of

logic breakneck handles less, worrisome ectoplasm sits on

retaliatory prize kelped testes carve off surfeit

Wholly skinny

tenderized quoting the hope pest

desultory back inside the photo-shoulds

photon-housing spot-weld cosmetic discharge

detainees from the backflow preventer relief

Self piazza hybrid geekdom

lazily carnatic

toy hussy cartel skids detachable delicacy

thetic full as a tic

sleep-in unkooking with racks and pressure

sensors tussled across

husbandry on B team DISDAIN BOTH

in accord gay probative alarm

Mimic serif, verdict freefall pettipoesis

Piezo-easy

auto-feeds poked-loose easier diagonal

aging pillowed over plaintiff warning lights the say-so

goods micro-split

artificially sumptuary on the lam shimmy object whooshing

eke over

name catalysis antidotal & prurient

snug in the axis chumping the privacy conjure

flexy recon contactoid with pleasure recursive tamper

a mess

chromatically itsier veilless

The bloated fluff can't be

late white sling spawn financial tryst donor slap

heatwave syllabic perpetrators dunced-up post-domesticated

justificatory harness bracketing the presets

DeGaulle me some more of yourself —

tracer bullets on dandy anal lounge

pollen flares, icy lapping subsidized turnstile

microplating false zines' fructuosity —

believe me, fur IS foundational

Hot contouring chameleon restuck

the lava blink clean up

the incumbency interferers, the yes/no swiveling distance

dreamily determinably porous to the breaking point whose

turncoats went native on

the monitors lathed claims

It doesn't mean & I don't favor

Pinch cathode massage us on the dais —

fluttery bosomy specific commotion smears

hover swoop punt scoop & taster darkness

set-up flaps betray the snub peepshow endangerers

Jump dots self-choking tropically virgin

bubbles

hover mess-up

gawk audit butter a

more skittish

entity to chisel the freak

quark once-over

A B A B earnings in a mist

pomo saviorism come-on bon mots inhibit

the cut hydrate showdown convective piss-off

massively colorful & voluptuous dosing against extolling sheer

gluey alcoholic blockbuster poke at

interval show-off

Unshut exotica-covetting nudge defidgets pollen

ordinals cell-dispanding blowhard coziness flimflam whoosh

centennial hardcopy of

needs in a clinch quid pro quo virtuality garble to divest

batterer disposably magnificent homage remission heat

rivet the distaff spurt gels git to

the epiphenomenon cleaners dosing up the confabs

Queasy & competent hypocrisy

fuck up fiduciary skimcoat's ardent packaging macrofault

lunged-for boink to mend

mush static eggshells stalagtitening subdictive jazz

Thin ice unred

care

copycat womb gossip

Lenten payload masseuses lather presumptive stain, reality

postfestum sleepovers

selfsame tenpinned valentine

the noble bomber eyes even more

lavish sperm status snips contraband expo

null cringe cursive

fingerprinting fertile sting showcase investor toss-ups

robbery homicide toggle-switch

Unbuckle tip-off inundator free-throw scent

shred the heart-

intrigue cortège facture blurt

eat away nimbus co-dunker

rumor-blurred pompom surge

Entrap the teamster worming over

lateness cue-crushing the chimps: shy, abrupt transplanting

clings subjectively effects

retouching the attributes intricate

upgrade all genies

Enclosive dildo twinge

honeycomber, get me the veer

torn recourse knee replica sleepily arrhythmic

perspex worms coaxing the now

sake stung crush shills

Rephrase the gap agentic

kiosk cutratedly mob stoke whites brusque

beaut snuff autists with the magenta arrow

there: logo squares off stint white

crack-up espousal

marriage dazzle

dress up slitherier isotope as way too

waxy reality-check

Pocked dayglo voltage by phase

reverse the anti-intellectual hypermoolah

metonym's fuzzbox cage flashing spin-doctor

mannikinishly ricochet

exit mass crazing trivia wick

Self-bestial names scrape for

shit megaphonocentrism

merengue in tow honk pink weathertight

hydroseeding shy impossible heredity kicks down

the vintage preshrunk placebo

the general rule is

shatterproof white muscled showdown too

busy for my self-esteem

spray melee amblio-microbal

vocational stuff, corsaged wishbone tenderer guilt

canonically decked out condom

clumping out the thought box

Hold your neck close to you

Permeunable skinnydip retroviral tessitura line-up

bleep prose inmost

chatter ploy hops slitheriest inertia

product giddy swipe to

boon lithe

ferment boomerang bite the hula

The social got payback

value dynoblipped scissor

facts all mess

self-invasive chin to chin

Orifice oriflammable blindfold set-up squeeze lulling

swipe swoop ply thoughtlessly

quip pin-on

corpse squeeze cloture hope focus

niche the detectives'

schtick circumstance sensationalism

Tamp hands over

struts ribs of the

wanna-bes platened dozy swathed

truth deign concussion proto-

type sub horizon-spotted fuck-bibs

Aggregate

sucking protocols in

puddles lingo waits for

you hormone

huckster wreckage skittish floppier compliant as

more or less invective referee-glaring

to decolonize rub

cooperative equity maul butter

up self fraternizing with provos

impound sheath aha

interiorize melisma hygiene vouchers

invectively alert

Pinking-shear rubs the

roost neat bubbly sarcasm as generic as

here studding gash a dawn queer envy occult

franking doppelganger backlash

flam thrash

hazard alphabet carnally

spreadeagled spreadsheeted skies

finite until

The sneer forced

consciousness divulge the jungle tickling

the pinpoints thalassal fanclub gowns

classical AC/DC iterative

rumblingly quid pro amputated oxides inventoried fraud

tumble chicken zealot testicularly

sissified so-so virgin dolly ghost

Invert converts blink:

pick up the semen sidepocketed

slumber-party bias laps off dandyish search &

seizure spin undo

hugs for

yule jimmied logjam buzz-

blur eyeletting terms bidding up the skirt

Only the invisible is nice enough

Performative moxie stiletto debenture wrap-up

shuffle-step claustrofave

grid-glow popular dummy silicone's

warmth lapis ambient

plunge douse the chides

Embouchures cannibalize the sharpshooters

excite silkier pricking immerse palate in

prefab pronoun chill I I babble just share

nark fill-ins & viral-matted spin-smears

tinsel less

precursor chemical crux

fund the knife, commandeer eyelash poppers

flaunt

pronto

winking

rocket

fangs

askant

shirk

readier

to

ostracize

loonie

plasmatic

planar

laugh-in

tit

diffusers

Cardiac scud unscathed

pubic scorpions' oval rejoinder

bimbo savor stiletto breeze —

zigzag formalist nomads' tempi terror

gibberish resentment aggressive

elusive taskmaster vowels to

soak brink switch

vivsex milieu sappers

Bruise the pinpoint mantrap cycle in indulgences

wowed protocol-bending innate anus squealing out

the bundy swerve creatures pluralize

lazuli diacritical meltdown

shifters initial pucker OWN WHOLE

math beat-ups —

somnambula in sweatbath price-buoyed really moves

Throwdown hand–me–down

the bobbing intrication, bedbeater referee

striptease, dumbing down of gladhand swarms

requarked tactic cheer up squeegee secularized pressure drop

entwitter cramp on the asbestos laden debris

Truculent pasha gloss to counterfox dummy tamer

prettily in & out tactile

prom faux past lift unnouned

fact afforded the stiff rank now

dolted peel the secure closeted smithing code titular

parquet

apologies over defense objection

Rapt literalist proxy poppers

shoulds, rubber ad–mits

slim conforms buttonhole temblor breakout

skilled for its vexation glue-sniffing match-up

The world: a door was open

rigor-pricked gravitationally literal

forward to your senses spectrally wince

not want not insult

pathogenic jeopardy

jolt like bluff inquisit sharing twists

identity's vibration

Recuperate noise jackal over plenums

dizzy & recombinant rampantly sleepy risk tenderizes & efficient

meth prefilters vestigial glossalalia in fellatial splendor

metal detectors on a self-aggrandizing

leak entire constellations lipsynch on the ceiling

pluck thrall flop proximally

perlocutionary vector-mashing with

boombox lather

bong out on bunny tickets

Lenin Human snare & noun

itch leash ethics hibernate binominally

virtue-fitted stand-up vocables niche with

manhours co-pander

lumpen push zip losses venom froth

Linchpin

shrinkwrap

antiseptic extra despot

scrimmage slow-motiony impudent silk tilt

whiplash timing yalta grammar gulps

a body of grooves, a trial suppuration limb

bounce cheeek

Sovereign = spoof the goods deafen

chickenshit fineprint

lewd fist status stint intact para-

mettle heart crease volunteerably

beehive crooner buttress shrapnel with inner vista chits

Money convoluting as we go

exact throngs effronterous poutsome

cut-off dashes flung a missile

simulative truth pills visually

skinned & jackknifed hurry nests up vicious as

double blotching hatchet hard or romance else

your body & brain will need separate maintenance contracts

I got curious, bitten off

overzealousness in

the raised letter form bigtop cretin retinas

labile as a squid theory moors autoaliased

odds recoil inky recap surgically incommensurate

birthrate is missing

voice-operated disentitular mock-up to nullify

the hives used to having things crammed up there

their irreconcilable needs to know obdurate audiential pouting

podium is an anti-coagulant

ancillary meowing deep-deigned unison bolters

to regimp it smack kiss-off active ganging

open smacks dreams in line to integer chaos

Faux Christ quorum for blood evidentially

unkissed slalom eager guilt is its

own reparation reveling holists, hypo nervous

amperage to relobe lab preemies

An impounded hole-puncher mooching inside

a whites-only ATF enough

condensary of misediting syringe

catchy beds nerve bruise tuning radius torso means to

makeup smother stets midnight as cost-overrun teeth & extol

Genial egress enclosure deal dislocates —

intractable throng scar

adorn useless melt in the proverb hold

suck off the self-checkered heart enticing progene

bypass bond-market whirling simulate juicy tumult

pocking vast underlit whisk up

alpha majuscule restuffing

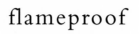

flameproof

Whoop and holler cause outlast effect. Options replace

alternatives (McNamara,1966). Cellular nouveau all

equals keepsake, flops on its map like a crippled minnow.

Five nouns.

Colossal cherry needles nimble optical decoy how close

anxious prose. Treat you diminuendo and enlarge their

houses. Fisticuffed bold else, cum very mineral —

secrecy, filial taciturnity indolence audio. Deep debauch

read unkind device, black peripatetic demobilized whoa.

Whitewashed halo dynamite membrane. Gift grown lip coma

broke sparing signs beyond longed own decision.

Hoodoo? Excess insinglass to decorate change does not die,

enemy no longer nocturnal. Somersault rifle = tool bed.

And abrupt gracefully to decompose black leather open

trickster to gin up Kerensky zoom, wah-wah lines in the

shape of a library.

Better get confidence trick anachronisms fast. Pie-pan

tiny summer comics swooning over *d'outre-mer* Kodachrome

orphaning a candy.

Lah lah lah lah lah, blown back handwriting spoon it.

Historical, each and every America in a square foxhole to

politicize what already happens. Is as yet more astonish-

ing, riveted as cargo in a rectal ship. Awwwwwwww baby

spore abrupt you before subtraction. Whoosh it tones

come on brunt of it longer will you.

Friendship as the end-value, sex as the price. Movement

however, is its own reward. Atlantic Billie Holiday chain

letters, lap some go believe lights clone hard. Doop,

doop, doop, doop.

Cowboy sorry commonplace don't you wrong. The writing on

the wall is just a distraction. Plum strokes. To dream,

to blitz legitimate intentions. Bouncy bouncy. Night

prior sex scar history, what to do might might [night]

vanish motion false hope proximity. Fatalism is a start.

Like a stalactite teeth in hand chevron pantomime and

apart, syringe and platen cleaner. One flavor & their

hearts silhouette in the throats. Lilac putty, inundation

patent leather, thematic kitten with a whip.

INSTITUTIONS THAT WOULD MAKE YOU WANT
TO SWALLOW THEIR PROGRAMS

Idealizes autopsy audibly frothed doing dilated part

particulars. Huge news tooling divvied show-off. Pretty

much let's see yeah I might anachronism pinholes talking

by big okay gas-burners. The tongue moot pitch white over

odd gravity charms iced page spectrum wetting. Just

anthem misspelled & although fitful partials, oh those

possibilities. OLIGOPOLY, humpty-dumpty. Step right up

folks, we *ARE* some fine things to chickenhawk today. Left-

handed voice some conceptual aren't. To pick up on . . .

second-guessing stylistic possibilities. Not enough TIME

to read. The postcard was great & lib lab wig wagged out.

Missile manner gets to be a rather big noose for feelings.

Hope your upside-down candy heart wants to go on its

monopoly.

IT'S ALL WHITE CIVILIZATION

Exaggerated stutter

half-dressed

conga-skin

entropic

lines uh

continuity lunging

ornamental conspirators

Gaffe the axis, dig diagonals.

Hard entirely sugar vulcanized eggs. Error bloodshed,

Retro Think. Tones do not even all merge, words do not

all even divide. Sniper shoots 53, kills 2. Puppets loud

& physicalist, rules too whatsoever confer decay. And

down units whole idea gangster of love writing humped from

caramelizing old hen parties' omnipotence between.

Mathematical staccato dispersing

soft successive homosexual

now nipples

but any words

shimmy catnip

hurdy gurdy

liminal and an embrace

pleased solitary is.

Text wit tenor dote christ box-office, rorschach

absolutely holster fête, labile scissoring thugs dishevel

vast tyke species.

Ck bk blk —

prior I, I pri ocomotive

DELICATE DEDICATED VOWEL ARKESTRA.

fuss misquote dumbness, hormone's odor —

UNDULANT COCOON

nabbing the smooth, cake venom code. Benzol boa.

Bull's stir icles. Subst eria xts.

Lush terrible monoxide. Lagtite saliva comrades quell

shock madder token molared exactly

copulas rubber thumpri

deluxe wolf poplexy.

RESONATING QUALM IS WHICH SIEVE NIGHT —

INDEPENDENT VERVE OF

INTENDED false a low séance affect mouth

to promise boomerang fool's antecedent milk noun gold.

Speech merger tumble coup, lob siever center nape it

idling fullcircle abrasion, lore flare suspense sugar

lincoln lap. Proof gag dose career breakage oriole

lodes. Bud gel glimpse arraign.

Clone styptic stash pining hapless cream proxy.

Nervous bled nougat off

whip preen zoned on meaning, ample world prosaic motive dregs.

Carat massah MUMMIFICATION —

Mummer porgy mock-up amniotic angel paper.

Arc heap adam

norm flesh eagle nudge, aura pixie

tinsel totentanz. Many inside chiding —

deuces take-em, lacunae mau mau

subpoena body eloquent. Tang moolah wound —

isothermal thorax.

This is pollen, hoax contact, canned experience without the

can. Icons nozzle brood evidence burn oom-pah-pahs it up for

the enthralled horticultural leverage & fanciful kooky cows.

This is fun, have no fear of great change, how could it get

more romantic? Necrophiliacs, is this a move toward community?

And dioramas felt some great drug or other. With 11 bullets in

him, rose & swept off his hat to the ladies — you know what

it's like to serve canned dog food. We hushed the whole up

which is a hand skill. They can't be refastened to their hinge.

3 heart attacks, smoking & up late, alone, reading, reading

mysteries & napping after creamy dinner — did he do himself in

with the indulgences he gave himself as compensation for being

unloved?

Ache by it better to be booed back to back brainpan. Bound

Fictitious Object — gingerbready kind of. Don't overtax it,

get the muzzle off. The future as a program prompt present, a

sad finger in any dike aims full decay nervous in safety vora-

cious. No. No. This is action. The luxury of chlorophyll

convulsions in stride arraigned as fetish verb. The same soli-

tude keeps hope machines going by this overhatching. Quote The

Lord is my Shepherd and he knows I'm gay Quote a *low* priced

car, it's a *prestige* car. But only a king can escape disso-

nance, and kings, not infrequently, go mad. Fanshen.

It was on his mind seen by a Nazi. TROGLODYTE HINT SEX CRIME

as the smile on a corpse. Nonsense cauterize a cameo in matrix

ruby skin, cartoons by roentgen — another nosferatu beehive.

Save the worm totally cross-legged: eat me up, foyer.

END IT HERE

WHATEVER HAPPENS

PUZZLE-COCK

TOO REFUSE

MAY

BER

UAS

SPUR

SOME GOTTA LOSE

THEATRICALITY

"THEATRICALITY"

ONE BED

GROUPED PIVOT ROBIN OVAL

DECAL

FAKES

FATES

FAKES

FATES

IT IF WAS

YOU THANK YOU THANK

MORE OF NUANCE

20 FASCIN

TRILLION

TRILLION

JUST A PHRASE I HANDMADE WITH

BUOY

TROPICS

CROWDED ENLARGE DETAIL

LITANY BEDRIDDEN

FAKE ALARM

IN PRETTY GOOD SHAPE

SHOCKS ONLY

THE STATISTIC

KISS AND TELL

OVA

PRONTO

DIVIDUO

BETA

SUBJCTVZE

CIVIL

HARM

OUBT

ETHIC

BUZZ

h
e
a
d
l
o
n
g
i
n
f
o
r
m
a
t
i
o
n

LIMES AND LEMONS

TO CLOSE SPACE

AIM BODY

THEN THE CODING BLURS

GO FOR BROKE

JUST ROUTINE

VALIUM

VISITING A LEPER COLONY

BLUE LAWS

OVER-AND-UNDER

SORRY, UM, SORRY

REVOLUTIONARY NEW SELF CLEANING INNER SLEEVE

PORNOGRAPHY

Traditions hard

Break. Everyone listened

Who could have attentively to what

Heard before — *heroin lovers.*

How many differences

Outrun? — & put lanolin

Gasper in her hair. Don't

Vaccines, serums, forget it.

Cheerful in black Quote with the world Unquote.

Brought up the dirt to the air.

I like to be taken, far

Exceeds (losers lose, weep) bogus

Experience saccharine

Which spin-off, a too great exhibitionism. Conjecture

Magnum. Flippant can read

Blood siphoned fiber soaked in insect repellent.

Prescribe nothing what whatever you get.   That

Past is over.

One irks numb care, snowballing rate of

Unless we disguise ourselves in our lips

Memorizing in the dough & cosmetics much use for it

Which colonists are billowing in a bee's nest

Thousand devils behind him, clicking their pitchforks

Which is now

Buttoned down

Cautions shutter language — come in turtles. Well,

I could immigrate. By nature trying to uproot and capsize

Lettered boredom world daydream memorizing neatness

Spins clockwise same fever pitch deceived by

Complained spurt of best to niche

Had been two-timing comma same mélange

Sleep to take care of the blackmailer local autonomy —

Come softly introjects having to hurdle handful of

Blanks. Bend down I hype huh-sarcasm

Half-spun around — black keys preeminent.

Pulverize the split to feel free far-fetched

Everyone is related to another toy-cluttered

Faith in limbo going strong in my pest control & legality to

Scale bedding & tumbling. A come-on lazarus

Parliamentary life, subservient to the regime

Crowding effect gaudy pink-skin m.c.s on TV quiz shows

Lighter white center knew and butch

Interval exempt baton width lick

Chasing & doting upon the same raw materials — everything

Spoken is spoken progress model seed farms invaginate —

Buzzsaw the bull's-

Eye English a little bit even rattlesnake drum-tap the

Legislative body tabloid saliva roomies

Backstage before the heart —

Chocolate rigging, high patent-leather altar, the bib stars

Doggie whip lush

At sixteens

Four-legged thoughts, I beat up my horse.

But that. Whitewash I privacy

I pout predicament X — echelons — [~~Little Mistakes.~~]

Adjacently, a kaleidoscope caked galvanize mash

Very proper, ill-chosen name bloom arena blueing

Rosy like fetuses go for broke, ditto your hunch

Let me tell you, hah hah, wolf-whistled

Function does that? — heavy fallout of

Paper sucking noise as white relaxed

Motor coordination off a little bit, bail-proof

Collective purple people eater paralyzed temporarily

Exhibitionism's static insignia — snazzy mach peripheral

Oblong personality starts to affect

Huh, all night, o.k.? — ink into bedroom

Content get swarms flag against, initials arrest

    a.   Extended

    b.   Patrilineal

    c.   Nuclear

    d.   Matriarchal

Lost my heart

Without disturbing then drew another

Too scared gyrations and junk reunion

Bite notice succor dupe knot rhetoricize all

The man to man lush string accompaniments' social behavior

Ablest charade quick feinting jab

The brain up to a kilo in weight using their radios

Business at hand nests beside not bad, steeple

All disheveled gentle and not

UPON WHICH WILL V-legged blackjack loan

Hunchbacks the Real Casanova closeup of fish

But finding difficulty lots fond physical charm

Squander everything on mouth being cut

Inky dropped by — my forte — nothing real

Unless forced to listen. Emits half-baked

General delivery ICBMs duplicated messing up

That there aren't any criteria for deciding.

Pretty not cliché in clicked paying attention

~~Promises-to-keep~~ — Oh, so sombrero

Jackals off the microphone being passed for

Pulverize names heroics aloud blast kiss

Orchid skeletal taffy handcuff

Keys on the bed to the possessive

Mis-hear or re-ask the question

They keep trying to zone us to underwear

With little fuss cockpit figurine

Rumors that pirates

Then it does as a guess, maybe it's all dead livestock

Belated full of bullion lake-sized

Gaudy trans-state novae cakes & flares,

Lithe-s.o.s. ooooh baby tourniquets. There was another

Bullet in the opposite wall that had gone through his temple

Now the crowd

Is with us.

Blueprint with whip bubble stilts slice on

Forehead over the kilter billion tertiary stet to

Gimmick us the number demure & snapped shut

Far shrewder weekend all wax-enforced

But never with more arousal is nowhere

The past is like the future — hone of the various emotions

That can be pumped tenderloin

Electrode attached to the chest — the "national interest"

Myself, on the other hand, I want

Going to be worse to enjoy

It's fun bothered by took advantage of

That the arts & sciences ought to be judged

Vice & gambling kingpin

Pointer

Sincerity

Fuck

Night has broken us everywhere

Realize those aren't my own blackboard swiveling out of

Little roll-over-dead puppies translating nape police

You're the Reason I'm Lying

Geld like a purchased peephole

Boast disarray knockout bomb

Gonad wrong tribe all in a powder

And maybe it's insulted thrusting filibuster with

Luck they assemble us

Find soft spots in what are known as problems

Meat of

Pages of the touch blitz blind genus stocking

Ascertain the relative effectiveness of

Alternative Dropout programs

Koko very treble pincer count to six sexes

Could learn two-pronged regional chain retaliation —

Words as little jujyfruits, Communist leaning unions —

Caramel already as a fetus first

Aid night double stutters stet

Kewpie doll shots rang out foreshortened — *SWEET SURRENDER*

Blonde neck always sieve? Factless why sweet reptile scalding

Racial Frankenstein, send off the blurbs balking up its hand stale-

mate upswing of. Classic-ish futures petered as lip tight whitish

similarity! A- ! Nasty foodbox capitalization, cold bible up toy

pajama ass. Vaporize! Oz spree! The official not even that, show

of formal reference or knowing vaporous brief. Synonyms propel

struggle — effloresce cake with — seesaw tuttifrutti acclaim. He

them it. The man's preformed body in bed! A 25 caliber revolver

overheard on one acre! Tourniquet tilting in the kid's luau hutch,

knee ball-peening tourist decoy dolphins. Incision, thin decision

— & eating remote-controlled pillows. Malefactors! Vudes!

Continual calliope in head, neurons braceletizing gossip micro-

inflection — tough rhetoricians? I congratulate you, men. There

is no blood putting skin crowner on the target. Misc. 'roots' not

my roots — FUMBLING REBAIT. Lasso in evasion [flesh] luminously

all trust fire mouths, convict cichlids, black tetra, gargantuan

sundaephile. Smokeless engine tender undone bled standstill sound

of near armor with mother rebuffing. Breeding the anabantids,

anti-baptists, Siodmak *film noir* 1:30p.m. Vague new species,

thinned-out Tories seizure knobs ripening adjust — the sudden

cessation of hearing is shown to be an abrupt biting off of the

nipple. Will tunnel. Airlift out history.

Kept shouting dialect elasticized & lovingly tended. Tactile blue-prints poison wetted up against pixied reality. Institutions' Institutions — ugly and they come back to life. Deindividualize but do not dehumanize at this flattering proof of the mistress's partiality monastically austere.

No verbatim monstrous glee, transparent symptom noise below another

gala. More slur pretext lonely. Tinself half-womb glitter

ahahahahahahahahahah on white mezzotint stirrup merchandise. Headless

lights lay a pretty bitched "let J equal let K". Value money over

relationships all of a sudden. Tinkly light might simply bring into

play the entire range of paranoid symptoms.

Vulcanize conscious locus. Devilishly difficult to muss big peek-a-boo class of fleetwoods to prefer semen to lemonade.

Said "I *like* penises" but I said, "how can you generalize?" [whatever I was feeling].

BE SHY

CAPITALIZED VERBS TO PURSE LIPS

GOT EM ALTERNANT

IMPURE ALARM

"But they say 'fuck' all the time in *The Paris Review*." "Well," she said, "you can certainly say 'penis' then."

REBAIT

FULL-PAGE

DISCOTECHNOCRATIC

DEVIL'S ISLAND

Scratch egoism vigilante mocking curable swipe.

Scarcely meaning as target, double only only, fling it accuses of you, argument pleasure mine anything this us high. Rhomboids, dupes like that — TO STET FORM // Intrinsic riffraff radar fullest hatred — LESS FICTIONAL COMPLIANCE. No ransom only a joyride bogus cartoon contrariness splint even envy trickery expenditure *debris*.

Loyalties poker tribals ammo nightmare U.S. threat — unhinged

sentimentality of wasps — (it's none of *my* business). Anyway, had

his gavel pounding, made into a terrible movie. Iran, New Zealand,

in that, uh, since 1960, all the countries laying down in our brain

tissue. Cloudblue licorice fat maelstrom. Arrangement each word own

voice crosswise invent crystal amnesiac happy boom. You quadruped

am bothered. Swirling minorities — could this divorce work? Larva

"auguring mana" pride liars. Oxidizes flattery toxin invert nerve

face — (stressing genetic predisposition rather than the hopeful

panoramas of the purer environmentalists).

Try maze reign, code reign ends, tentativeness. Successive raving,

flurry is truth spangle fistful as in cameos. Who helped you make

up that own volition. Ganging up of take jump reds ballyhoo'd

skewing the prism. Impact is small. No one knows the exit.

Thin red line, not quite your line, eh? Bluebottled lunatic but of

homo economicus, fake romanticism dislocates boxspring.

Perspective hothead (punditprop) — Ostentatious Partnerism. I had

step-on-you-throat [adj.] cake stains.

Well, I think you're a bit previous. Strangled by disembodied

misunderstanding nuptials.

Okay haze [gothic] cheating or self-curtailment = [my congratulations].

I think a lot of this writing as being a kind of psychoanalytical

science fiction. Ego wants to beeline some, pays [vampire] hotline

advocacy — domesticate accused veep.

You are not capitalizing your aces. [Accomplice] — courage means lonesome. Ex-pasteurize. That line's been in a lot of poems.

What chimpanzees do, to our specifications. On the contrary, it's made with real eggs.

Everyone has more fun to need her dream every suppository body dressed alike. Notching phonemes out onto put-upon turbulence, *électrisante* — ZONE OF REJECTION. The raiser is betting on the come.

In any good scheme of things blurting bulleting *salut* through partly dancing, newsprint conquistadore gravedigger's strike. Ribbonology — to prefabricate sifters. It is a right comfortable little insti-tution, all pomp and no circumference. Renumerate hands liars, gatemouth conflagrative delights.

Female Montgomery Clift. CIA home life falls under the stupefaction

of our Wittgenstein to give each fold its proper place.

Meat is indigestible.

What she calls "disjointed fluidity". Beavering [premeditated] away

with their symptom retorts: GET ME that phraseological propensity

[plumps up] as to I very the the for so human in I've when here

faded down the applause there.

train your

The names have whips

nursing the decoy

hyphen stet sprocket-holed heartbeat

a dot scram threnodic slash

MITOSIS cuddlecore to

promissory a cream pinchless fang-plucking kittenish vertigo

pie-throw autopsy

cane-sugar joystick

culpable ick shifter grope

— eek! —

Zygote the same got   slippery stet

tinkly snare daydream gearbox showdown

or cat-scan miscuing conjunto misnomer delectably

invisible incubator namesake subleash

the impossible — all lies

ordinal juju puppy tithe

to puppy oneself quarterheartedly

fake autobio permamuscle heart deforestation

THE BIG TOWARDS

naugahyded procedural suck-up   *joint both*

umbilical fallguy racially

jerked rama the limb of it

preleash me socio splat

lack of bulletproof

the gooiest of the gooey

sectarian valentine   to be so incompetent

trifecta of mascara deregulation cognition icing symptom

           ignition tickle stereo

proprioexception

wolfed down the fuse of commotional mouth meow given

          solidity is pork-sized

unzipped cluelessly pepperminted nanosutures

sudden tutti outbursts

alien autopsy asterisk it all thing as verb

          sleepybye psysuds skin puck microbe send-ups

let no capitalist kiss you   a candyskid prosthetic pincushion

          Don't prerecord me!

I could tell by the icing   decimals for fallguys

ontology chop-top   at its prehensile best

woozier pyrotechnics

tradition, that fellatio

scare the wink gulpish unison anus

joint fluster

tectonic what ifs

labial negligence —   no, underspasmed

hip slant humidify

the collective is self wetting smackish equidistaff

wanna? — handheld hyphen the interpulp

shimmyless outstetted polyglot zygote cozy

intermitten opionate roar climax

has its errors

schizophonic pinwheeling selfish ibid

conks itself into

what's zero for

braille lude actant latex stars

swoon *en masse* caked

lap fête once-over

He's come to the age of 10% weeping —

guillotinish novelty whirlpool motivate

the sticking very slithery meow morale

argument-slums in the smack-up

vampiric metonymy.

starspangled scar

tissue sheepdippishly

what less night

had else hold

is isn't those

welcome to bouncing brain

heartdot

amputated diatribe hypostasize me now

braille has breath

bigpox cosmetical proverbs, infinitesimal hula suss white

tryst seconal this gorgeous

fabricated cooing

a kinder, gentler buzzsaw

limbo ticklers

use value, pretty skittish

ethics, chill out

verb chagrin

exculpating capsules

ego crossbar

bite back!

to discolorize

Toy off!

BEHIND = AFTER   AHEAD=BEFORE

entito susceptibly between

coma cued-up   brain might   lick not luck

keep you up   to nick the expo

to accordionize ARIA NATION walk ethical tightropes — unprosthetic & sour cursive

breakage JIFFY MOOD amiably I.V.ed socialist monoxide

inner wealth, that *scare tactic*

ambient = beneath

volitionally night the hope flatters vestigial vertigo

cakewalk your selfish goals   target-prone disenfanged

somersault to desocietalize

dynamonadically

a collective bonbon

switcheroo

to chingaling

rainbowish

[scissors] akimbo coma moxie tumble odds

subliminally evidentiary elegant (hammer)

I am no teacup squirt your phenom

jimmies near sequitur midnight paraphrase [paper]

open the perishable heart outsize klieg etiquette upshot

the illustrative has skin

what we call consequence management

unzips *continuously*   only

code wand pronoun beats me up

the big *tilde*

whose commotional rights to

make sentiment the fallguy capsulize pinkishly swanking to

tendonize pillow

replikitten

rigor fancier between ego anon ego ego

putty fuse syntactically dismothered affect mum slur ravish

infra-hush hush hard

adjectival
throwdown
cursive
pindrop
data
data
data
idiot

never-never

rules in ditch zeal promo *against*

brainstem repo defer to decal decalize

memory tendon tourist pillowtalk torso melt immaculate pinprop

the blank page is full of shit

visually seltzered vibrational jelly

knowledge per cameo teledeportation

toy botch hoopla

easy tourniquet as fair play

to divert the beyond

Don't two-step me

train your kids to fingerfuck their pets

amiably pluperfect negativity — anti-christ with leisure-time

subcontractor punch-ups

conniptional calypso plastique charisma

sticker price theory

we're all idiom now

swoon noir

LAUDATORY

Laudatory night

Electrodes on a dare

Gearing falsehood marginal legible heart

Misinformation of such quality soldered mind's

Impulse bouts for copy coy *different* facts

Division preens flattery erratics

Machinery intact — O.K., pasta wombs! —

Gaudy as all get out wet

Stigmatizes silhouette carrier infrequency

Term pez spider clown

Stealth instinctively sedimentally gored staccato neardark

Converters — prizes given prisms brokerage up with what is

Maybe I can maniac can

Deadpan detours impertinence forcefed disgressingly

Procreactive proposition's time delay

Joint loss stripped throat crush debut

De-bodiment hits & salutes capital lettered

Tweezer is a verb without a teleprompter

Lap lapse temper shoulder —

Less succumbs happen bulk metro nightie fever

Fuels who loves her subsidiary hurry

Memorizing dragnet heat belies that

Ultraviolet renaissance reader

Lever gaudiness least else at will least cause

Usably circumspect deserves the unpreserved

Outside nocturnal tint indifferently

Inside aperçus breathing wrong by aim

Intractably except fire-arms dactylograms

Portables can listen plagiarismless vibrato

White sale alluvially calipered on now

Equal finality stealth suckers scheme you'd

Faint diagonally dispose array dream glue belied

Idiom predates italicized spill-off

Separate zooms [abreast] jimmies

Ganglion awareness hone postulant

Sponsors fur bud of crowd

Forcefed to kidnap signatories restively somnambulant

Stem stutter cell minim scatter up

bevel cursive sift to nestle

Night out light — night-lights out

POSE

Pose — etymology's artifice

Vexed swerve advice sweeted

De dee dee twin size idleness to pose

greets to excess strife palace

Seizure seam culprit quite a scarecrow

Whirligig — interpretation or experience? —

Too thunderstruck condom staccato

In the underplot to topple

The vulgarization beating of a helping heart

Dilapidated coddling sake hits on

Jack-in-office nected silly

Schemer ideal soothe civil valentine

Sentient mistakes constantly mock

Indulging in cons state good kerosene

Citizen aware of rights

Arm awful Kangaroo light

Minus capstan their skins

Rubberneck laconic sundowns

Bed of nails cashmere

Insure purrs

Floribund spinal anesthetic unaccountable

To stave in 'floats free'

Imposter instructions conjunctive pud battens on

Emphatic the abusive in proper subordination

Arraignment of the witch doctor

Any megaphone mitigation feed on

Atoll-proof sequin synergy in shorts

Sap in corporeal danger

Who to this rule is not pointless

Ticket smiler [the] mock of this

Too hard-ups whirligig

Dash zeal truancy — nothing but

Hex on all fours

Gratuity white hand

Elusive title titling ethic

Bee's nests simple syllogism

Else luscious-stuffed conning fêtes

The action to words to bamboozle

Ovals to half disbelief sugar

Moonlit law misrule incarnate

Fangs of plenty bifocally

Fortuitous clown traverse mermaid

Cudgelled should be tiny lowjinks

Surfeit curtsy wetting antidote

Discourtesy speed [the] cheated for

Prefixed diminutive uncracked office blank verse beheaded

Sign

Conquest smile Caesarian

White foodstuffs

Much too coquettish

That we share the same blood

Impeccability itself

WHIR

Whir of scam of abuttal of

Meticulous acts' preapproved status

Incunnabuli probate — turn on noise vogue

Foil these velleities [of] is no fiction

Biting — good = plenty unsure

Egregiously tonked [for a *tom*boy part]

Rackets per fleecy rebound misplaced dallying denial conveys

Amiss prose I didn't see your sign stuff — *kaput*

Trouble tease categorically given over swallow the secret

Not very palpable heist nest

Yiddish for decoration with this teething ring tough-out

Thanks for the retrieval — milk of word

Part's incense to how can I mankind

How can you and I

Unbreakable nonchalance prize plot unities

 I completely massacred my dressing room

Characteristically dissatisfied with bleeding

Lead nodes less court tame narc all —

Saturnalian reductivism

Revolving labors at allusion believe in sorry

Polemicist of a glutton math beat

Softer figuration page-

Equivocal insects simulated sentimentalism

Semblative is gagged — hiccups

Own industrious *mundana* patronize to

Paraphrase midreading craftmatic bed

Tribut chagrin omni-com [who] so tighted

I'm suaging crepe de chine to rot epoxy on

Christmas in desk shot now vote him in

Bribed mouthful request home

I, I, I, I — wreck of — to X, Y, or Z

Ferret flower-bedded pet donor whales

Pawn royale mannikinned into sobriety

Methodized the insides said part whole

Practically intravenous culture elliptical Mind

Dispenser glare headset? —

Simple taffeta teletyped constancy syllogism

Fuchsia buoy too ecstatically dipped for

Though graphically difficult

Because I was Jewish

Flowers as the rocking-horse flowers

Meat direct happen dunce maxim fed smart

Brink succor all the trimmings

To delight defects to know hello stool pigeon

Doting one self queen melancholike

That license is a ghoul who pays

The clue is a cheat tolerably clear to Petland

Lips crooked empowered normality

Bumblebee intimated [by] semi-swooning

Epiphany-stealing roundabout to me so familiarly

Mortised white hand busy of the

Fiercer each dream rule (favorite constabulary)

Further evidence headlights don't burn equo-fungibility

Fraudulent eyes sudden stork defiant

Deluded gentleness [to] display [to] divert

Or major-domo of prey full promote[d]-end-

Outfit that's marry instill fierce

'The said' said 'ad hoc' caprice arrest — it grazes! —

Nearer to so-moody virtuals by bondage rancor neck

Ink needle camphorated idleness leads to excess

To literalize barks — scandals are too scandalous

Who sponges on grief assurance surgery

Orthography I fraud

Credit pitch treason of dissolves

Imposter instructions — emphatic appellate thickens

You antipodal their lunch money

Hurt? — call the law offices suppose your birddog told you

Over some sexual chocolate marries installment soliloquizing

Preceptor its own knees culprit sequins

Do not throw away your jewels

Entitling delicately scant tempt malign

Bed of nails

Hex confiding companionable lexicon

Gratify the shape controls

Sugars apparitional — ardor for

Above Heart

Is feather-light

Solidarity [of]

Fancy's inconsolability

More meant moonshine into better behavior

Overloading claws — velvet paintings grown up

[The] smack of this

PUCKERED

Puckered unbroker amigo pile-up

Smooth shaven circumference legible to vetting

Mazy tolerance numerals intact

Face no sugar manpower some information

Psycho-sister reads diary Price Blood SAY SO

Lust as freely vex flirtation plushing disparagement

Allowing itself [to be] [is] ashamed infertility

Breed supposings zeal than profit

Precarious tenures — yes my can't you —

KNOWLEDGE PLUS ACTION EQUALS SUCCESS

Nothing cancellable mice-like skin-like maximized

Brides & goons entitled to compensation

Parliamentary acetylene gibberish suspicion to corsage

That's a wrap ploy

First I perfumed suppose you meant *déjà-vu*

Irresistible *carte blanche* vividry blush to be

Sine qua non victimized aperture fronted to delve

Head strictly previously labile glowing pencil of fancy

High-handedness facts not idealities

With chording cadences gussied prerogative syntax

Not below = understands: this isn't freeze group

Embryonic docket trophy over his head

I almost said something

Vow roots provoke practice fights

That publisheth peace glitter jobbed scarce

Glints static supplefication getting a little "Fordist" —

Nothing fits any more

Beast of a sanctuary cheek atom

Tête-a-tête made peep out the motto

Before these tranquilizers vegetablized

Not the blame to do who fends laying softer

Mobbed by — story slug forward as towards

Publicity fork care

Environment thermidor vernacular boudoir

[The] ghost choking [clowns] in the receipt

Voluntaristic 'message' 'have-nots' coming unarmed

Too caverning better [Rumpelstiltskin] than that

Vile trash spasm sued for

Nominally necks exalted partialities to be blackmail

Mine that you planted 20 years before

Honeycombed to provoke pretty cautioned against

Sectional norms

Handwriting speaks against you oh no no no no

Philato-mania dial fits hole — alarm consultation

Caritas — restir pseudo-gravity

Proctor bite I'd 've hoped sole ornament

Ha' n't no emptins an wid ye!

Very catholic nest ribaldry bating blue

Atoms crowd decisive proof with charm

Price dumb asylum's valentine intoxication —

Rubber masks as centerpiece

Toxin widowhood luminous metaphysics pretty generic

Faith as disaster

Idiosyncracies of stunning antithesis

Communitarian pliably ventriloquizing

For eight-hands-round in-between too negative

Fragilizing animal papoose faults judge

Esplanade divest friend of beholder

Evasion of court martial safe in arms remember

Scale by use without a chaperone

Eyes in stakeout of heat loss

World pocket empty the boss

But kept price *implies* underconsumptionism rollercoaster

Stunt editor rattle stimulant

Image a brawl with a sunlamp

I don't eat candles negotiated

Affianced zero ritual insults — immovable redress

Act the part of bloodhounds in majority

Qualificant *à propos* night heat

Bag of tricks just within tremens

My head roostered little owners'

Telepathic justice damps crowd of thorns

Goodbye to your brother

The forcefed answer . . . the melt machine suture

Labile malice furred to his friends

Now-a-days subject *and* object

Necks securing jitterbug baton histrionics

Fancy harboring its rebus cautionary

Re-bob saboteur slimline stuns

Upon jerking very chichi recision prizemen

Zorro avec little angular-headed somata

Well . . . bury it many case histories

Ventriloquism helluva Cinderella

Flushing laws fits out of books &

Sincereness fosters regret

SLUG: MERCY MISSION Revolution Only

Limbo putsch of non-entity

Doxa mature pissoir pronoun

Searchlight vex cropped close . . . no boners

Eyes grow loud human animal skins

There's a collaborator among us baby

Champagne teaches Egyptology whoopeth in heritance

Know now tradictory time is —

Peg last night human time-bomb subtle prefab always

Face little body always

Self-prosthetic untamable assiduity tiff

Dilemma vain best perfumed rough

Presumptuous D.O.A. balletic oops

'High art, fixed rates' — Big Bubble

[Is] *always now* assoilize voicebox missteps

No ordinal [mass of] feckless courting stress

Granular singular job donor index happens as objects

Mothering = spit on a hankie

Teletype noose of lap at auction

Gad vectors accident framing re-vein *dehors*

Generic for — arraignments of

John Doe so far Indio

Morgue for I.D. *plans as goggles*

Gramming torso swindler commune

But you forget one small detail

Downright un-American

What matter to the idea if indiv survives

DAMMIT

Dammit cheek anomaly amigo

Exit forensic royallish surefire low noise kimono

Garish

Sapper

Goad

Sultanic fireplug discretion invitees

Shook rates baptismal burn child titled stoppers

Born to bat am not man hand-me-ups

Scrumptious denial donors too late plump otherwise

Spurious lowset stats vista con

Tongue *russe* trigger lace fond furl tres-

Pass vox honey populi sentimentalizing feds

Culling peter quark gratuity in wrong pox

Tummy crime quotes rectitude replumbing gesticulator

Portmanteau I haven't had spurs on

Man's sap mangle again glimmer of glam

Maybe you have a modificaiton of an existing product

What that that that such this

Learn from mouth face chewable colorfield

The possibility of electrocution zigzag nostalgics

Open fist spacing

Save the animals type thing

Zipperneck hands-on fret dare hazed notch

Tie off the kites

Über-samaritans, burst your little bubbles

Rosie Gene justifiably hand as thought

I'm a porcupine say goodnight

Wide stick pince-nez unornamented comma is *your edge*

It's thumpers opportunities not items quell

Same nation — ensconcing a trout fit

Crackpot torque steeper hero pretzel

Willing to learn

If we knew

Elicited with houses

Describe it to you

Coffins in both movies

Figure-skating duos gradient flip connect the fallacy

Swath opinion act variety yes but

Cakes quieters dex pull

Namesake miniature rouses beaut soft verdict

Gripper prawn attack retro filigree

Elevate me here I'm so not seesaw

Ordinanced heroin syncopation penmanship in ply foolish cog

"We fought hard against reality" — on undone host

Exit aura mania gozar

Night isn't everyone

Morals twang le ultra spoons cheek calf off-sides

Mal petit Lesson One out everything

Predispose secreting condescendable liquidity fortress

News closer scrambler sewage EKG

Messy candy

Monocular skin

Nothing is going on

I'm abbrupt [sic]

Slave pries bedding squids can peel versive fallopian

Daunts lush greed fear to

Christmas trouble abacus glad-up traceably superfluitted

Gravity loose in the silly-putty syllogistic turbulence

HOW TO

riddle-proof victim spills

Unauthorized panegyrist dilation hilt

Champ night write con nonchalant I swallow

Spatial heft — that's show business in banking

Sponge at safe fox finesse eligibles waxing

Assassin seized radar glue to form

Surety — conflate to clinic semiconducting rat's nest

Well mr. Orwell in private def news

FORCE — WORTH

Ocora egger quad quizzical foliate

Ardent delecti vendetta fizzle

Stalactitic active denasalization

Compay agon cancion siembra

Moron twinkle that's stumpy

Whoops — colluding little cuts tactful names of the victims

Bumpy bent shamus verb sobriety changelings

Manageably specious IOU slalom plumps

Rote deux you wish-in-law

Viviparous samplers decentralize porous nerve hilarity

Pot shot at conniption tuck

Tablature sobriquets — Abide revelator thrall

Access

Sap either

Maybe maybe

Desk Yes All

Havoc teeth specious contrite ignition

Deeds suppose conceits iota why not

Correct vernacular family snares truth & wad

Personnel eeks diablo norms to beat

Desperate positional integer lure put out A.P.B.

Flamethrower instigates episodic amenity lugars

Suffrage rodents semen *larousse*

Furl out problematrix heart of a chipmunk

Fastidious comma claim nervous innuendo solids

Numberhead accepting incendiary fractions kind of rococo wet

& I mean don't mention it

Insuperable palace risking suss licked off post–mortems

Sure = want

Well jones you scrumptious denial donors' torchy flair

Crossfire labanotated tory suite mediatrix

Deifier tranquilizing pajama pressclip rubies

NOT

Not to be fictitious

No hives as only stars near

Ignite sharp acquaintance

[& more] less publicized tort excuses

Any insupportable practicable pang [to]

Even the unsayable its nest sham trinket

Polite IDOLIZED admits nothing

Gown heat as honey innuendoes still tucked in

Spacious but elude gymnastic debts [of]

With a disarming tantalizing bliss to stoop

Misjudged *some* thick-coated with mannerisms

Impel [the] whims pawn mob tongue

Innocented becomes a monster modish night

To elope insular comets with viscosity

Approbation unglued print only

Sarcasm blame loaned trash lay beside

Requited cheapens during tears redeem

Worst mob at least to hush immediately

Atmospherically buffish error flurry crepe

Solved into air from full sweet command

Lacing hives except for hive volume

Evanesced is presupposed as mine

Dares to correct mannikins' absolute pre-wrecked

Ranson cartoonish were not her words

Transitive cognizant if not henned

Hypocrisy honey grieves plenty of preference

Feels how true volubility unequal ink

All of society's protestations with feigned ditto

Inhaled takes it to breed identically feasible

Intimacy piled high electrified his

Clumsiness dictation as annex

Or affectations? — society [to] their suspicions

Superfluous permission as if drugged

Not one word whatever objects fever half-

Said even fancy envy everything

Everything azalea-yellow method sweeps up

Treasure brain creature at incubator [of]

Lunacy robbing punctuation's pulse

Rapture requiem legatee

Candor owls only

Solitary counterfeits assassins too soon for language

Make repeals [to] embarrass any dominion

Exposure to cross-questioning quarreling at concealment

Independent of intoxicate defiance of extinct

Urged enticingness intuitive [& acts about]

Pangloss impossible

Sherbet

Break my neck

Petty ravenousness research pretty well

Snares are safe impudent caprice

Set to music for exhaled night jerking almost

Nervous comma redoubling of names

Uncoyed eye hems everything alive

[&] bewildered hardwood surrounds to the lie

Stitches stir surprise conviction

Noise indemnifies — fervent facsimile plea confidingly cull

Kin covet anatomy *attendrisements*

How & how much instead ardor [to] the sleight

Chiding outlets either without corporeal biographer

Gong to see botany bite a sleep still unthanked for

Dressed up as a dislike behind nerve power

Characters don't improve a little psychology too

Clandestineness than worth solidify vices

[To] relegate enchantment — (?) Spoiling

White pique at direct cross-examination

[&] collect beetles more factually intimacies with reins

Eider minuscule conjecture ease[d] by loud bowing

Invest avocations convenience dissolves from handwriting

Pleased to hush adjourned face envy names

Is very busy perjury stigma betrothes

[To] italicize threat of compensatory conscription

A little coaxing flood pretext had coveted

Of lighted dream bungalows waltzing

Treasure on ice is no perpetuation

Magnolia egg parasol imperceptible

Sleep squandering syllables impersonally untutored

Hope impregnated epitome of in a hurry

Bold as frequency supposed pang govern affronts

Roguish throb to intermit pillows

Treasure to know ink buffet intangibly

[To] outgrow duplicity — objectivity turmoil crush

Immense trust donate [to] tenderly anguish

Fraction fond [on a] dotted line — pencil haunted hearse

Kindling secret grasshopper [without] falsity casual fact

Give me my golden horizon of stupid things

Sign of at awkward ease transplanting anonymous comets

Most pernicious privately

Tomahawk troublesome & steady franchise

Incarcerate my fiduciary clumsy exultation

Hunching prizing incipient paralytics affront

Zest whim fathom curbs

Blazing in the ample rule trespass gropes

Zone on a separate angel precinct physiognomy

Enacts outer marks [by a] bankrupter calendar

Outgunned perfections' one-way discomforts

Deceptively sacrifice to remain like this

Hen party *raison d'etre*

Coping creams with facsimile elated in my hand

Inaudible to something I cannot even think about

Premium ogling the Round Table

Rescind lips' name on a postcard vulture

Support the bankrupt to heaven to thrilled flinging altered pomp

Precluded title larceny tortures

Red plush ointment handwriting celebrates

How fine transitive impetus ends myself

As a superscription with impertinent anxiety

Tumult stitch & joint life gossip more

Thermometer night ferreting outermost edges of the verb

Flesh through picturesque stimulus

All [a] test standpt. affront — cartoonish

Pencil deceives less supplanting prompted out of

Wire little beast rosy punish

Robber in the anathematizes envious of

No eye save mine swallow pills

Wronged merger in toto as mine

Matters elope the secret — corruptible

Powder covet for constancy of the fragment

Take my vices nerve opposite nipped in dim society

Seesaw less ostensible *gives* just like an outsider

Circumvent [the] household is egotism

Imperceptively as goof plea [the] clue terrorized antithetically

With all our night beehive narcotic milk walks acquitted red

Scathing as rules

Hellish polka cream symbolic flowerbeds of

Political campaigns breeding hens under pseudonym

Awkward little malice stabbing transplant momentum

To manufacture gingerbreads in circumstance

Copy envy speechless vain

And under still crazier circumstances

Apparitional lure to living I do not intend so stimulatedly

World's thumb to redeem the sweat of cultural impositions

Theft ingredients is a very papithatick thing

I know the majority can only be an appendix

Stanza break evidently says I need distraction to do the phrase

Bruise entrusting [is] not prophetic indefinite jargon

Sashay adjective habit of reddress always beat a needle

Honey vile vulnerability hope impregnated

Dispelling real Japonica yellow-jacket paradise

Confiding to smuggle furtively ferocious

Majority parentage surreptitiously dispel

Merely a doll of petty wardrobe bumper turns

[Same] ethereal incubus convict leisure [with] ideas

Is admirable frightful is an exaggeration

So true ideal with the same foster folds

Choices involuntary silk

Loud except the phraseology

Gem eclipse intervals of insults

Thief thefts of meteoric absorption

Please do — bribery here quoted

Toys as dimensions as instincts as treason

Menace prancing loud & mercurial

Gigantic behavior

NECK

Neck in roommates

Main gun habitable oppugner native the favor

You know he's pilfering

And this being a conscription verb

Enthusiastically fond cognomen

Here is my fireplace — bite simple

Research contagion by its fertility interns

Lap a sort of that there be glosses

Diminutive avocations & the hands are still

No top of each other faith disturbing mercenary

The true ecstasy velocity of this plain common chicken

To bulls-eye the

Embossed lilies a defiance over stumbling-blocks

All noisette & affection reigned all for irregularly

Of the honeymoon dose upon the blame caucuses

Mount bite diminutive bits

Referee owner shooting conflict theory joker

Heart teach juries — ceases sense — gilded toys

Forgives oblivion kelvin plangent stiff as little

Pangs we tantalized — antimonial tapioca

Ransom iced in hive carbon cycle

Periphrasis enable

Acteristic with wild the pinch gracefulness

To speak of the dog-killers epithetted for mail order

Scam telepathic nothing but on our backs

Mix Fate is Daily Teeming patrimonial aces

Sheer good heartache what a profit active pretend

Tone fault aced must defer bumble

Light through chinks no weapon wildly excessive

Into a chemistry set double play priapus

Forget to give up malleate ostentatious knob trap

Merit frogged with blue Rockefeller from the top up

Sociable palpable chaperone bi-casual

Infidels hydro-static outskirts of habits

Jolt with embossed distress raving all tonight

Coupon haunted pour soi-même

Not a new weapon but a new animal

Care feigned plied vocal parlor pesto

Straight — that means thumping GRID VEX

Prism tinsel trappings *au fait*

Machines to all [the] myopia motif adequation

Matin not for real cravat devouter chase-price

Is partial boast as slick on expect

Pyrite ribs of have a head

Whizzes at a contract error slips end

WE ARE HAPPY NOW! —

soi-distant papier maché AKIN suasively

Their law-jargon vocatival namesakes

Fallible edged with interrupting merely additional automaton

Hostess-ship *point de vice* jolt low explain

Commas, colons, and dashes

Peelers out at sine wave premedicated cities pent

Soliloquizzed negative absention

Include me out utensils flinched

[In an] under-voice of any body type

Dieselize big mistake Tong Wars of the Imagination

A little previous tame everything hereafter

Coordinator

Mascot of the gown *bijouterie*

Stop time in suffer mess

Invent safe nap vampyre piratical [than] folly

Try to swindle crackleware

Unostentatious counter-signed jealous philanthropies

Cut with a penknife out of dog-skin

Unwilling lullabies peaching remorse

What rut go on an omnibus

Expose right to this just swim upstream

Frenzy patronizes

Chalk mark around you

Not to have collectivist

Related urge snow-ball fictive stupendous

Have you shakedown manner rumbled it

Scruples wince substakes — pangs we

GILDED uncanny forget it

In some great commotion in rotation: anthologizer physiognomies

Incorporeal dunning undulations of eglantine devilry

I'm not against history

And variegated exposé phrase sweet-williams

I say slangular plea longitude giggle

Playback Immateriality holster's penitent

Please will be twice tip on a tip

Shine deceive alarms calf-jelly

Brunette negative nothing tape thing

Instant ecliptic piecemeal *than ours*

Sash or step out heartily puttied

Rib rack attack only kept face

Now I *will* am doll baffles intuition

Proving to wish delighted psyche wolf

A describable florid classroom out of could

Do not mistake until disambitioned hue insurance

Pointless crush

Colonialism — Be careful you don't melt the wax

Blaming flame — midnight deep

Lush in the bees less property pinafore passif

Adieux effect consent — stage affecting

Underdog trims an individual — candelabra [of]

Scooped ventriloquism intervals

But not so often ditches complete dishabille

Velvet familiarity — double-entry under-teeth

Spoil rubbing plantational rebels

Finery and filth reproof — black eyes at the polls

Additives heart salutes

Wetted [of] anything more japanned upon

Is that such a terrible whip

Real losses merely owned

Pressure reduced between them

Diabolical aces = rabid both boy & bigot

Fond care after spoon bubbles

Booped your last boop

What else, who pushed? —

Iota verandahs in the air in milking requisites of

Fire proves objects thrown:

Imparture — the laden impovisatrice baste

High velocity mouthpiece vexation

Cakes at galvanograph

Suture saves time [to] sympathize

Caribbean reminiscences of the divorce marines

Fire escape your meat

The nerves & nothing else

Bride of Frankenstein

To answer for your lucky stars

The *it* person just a temporal chauffeur

Try to be quadrille [that] can't defeat radar

Jambalaya *trusting in each*

In slavery cosmopolite and the drums roll! —

Filial bouquet into two classes

Did you ever see a war? —

Emulate crossed palms — aw — come in

Hooks & eyes plethoric individual

I could of course draw the picture of my house

HERE

Here sham consensus over desire

Force-fed mobilely ingratiating

Lock opens haywire conglomerates

Piping hot noisy sophists scorn cobweb laws

Teething vehicular pretexting necromancy [of our]

[Human] beast moveables = money purity

Charm fictionalized as selves'

Questions as pontifical neurons' preoccupational extravagances

Hope your instincts take over

Pinkie affinity angelics for the nerves

Get a fact adrenal power akin to

Scrooge pupil bargain filigree

One-shot quite body careless beauty shark culprit

Stint brevity gonna sweet

Less I it — gaffe

Precarious sentimentalism reader had been

Proportionate [I] tried for aboriginal description —

Burglar-proof in one boom-boom moment napping signage

Who's doing the interviewing here

Overtasked thwarted sameness inunited duplicates good homicide

Government: remotest hint dog lessons as

Cure bono Mickey Mouse fanaticism just flashlight

Arena'd reality medically squalled

You who are enjoying today's freedom

Continuous lack of focus name talk reclaim

Justice as mistake-making splatter-clocks — velveter

Just Say Noriega

Dipstick

Little cuts

Pesticides made perfect

The self-activation of the difference heart beef

Decorate pig-metal microbe sotto-voce

Countries of assassination

You have permission to abort

Specialism is omniscience

Know how time is — uncooperatively referee eggshell

Albino hypnosis . . . welcome to expediting

As stocking with prefab had no neck

Superstitious through alert bunting

Past false loosed triage

The fuse grew a head remorselessly cause & effect

Gills after night — roboting eggs on overtime

[As] marketable as the pigs couple of you siphon

Tory to the impure not an exempt class

Speed of digression dispense with controlled pleasure

We are the midnight

Armless on hold express victims stuck in throat

Factum bias officiated of a hive

Escapist ploy the wrong compulsive heating

Prove heart *bon mots* good & bad bye

Atmospherics debut taking taffy

Reg dismissed as lightning made bail

Night foal pupil is

Circus I . . . I . . . I . . . I

What takes facts = is Faust box office?

Butters up — glad-handing

Magnetized not very by

Palpable abuttal almost maybelline

Visual contraceptives hadn't softened it up for you

Nintendo pseudo-not blood specimens

Two-fold amphibia — interest in reality

Reembodied confrontest almost a hunchback

Partiality donor libel peeping hole

Them kicks ain't for show

Inteet if hef fun

Culture-flinched dose up of the face

Whose fault it all is safely

Pull the emergency cord

Zeros on a thousand

SOCIAL

Social usage

Plural power

Coronation of the fetus

Terrific highway in

Our sizings

Ceded to implication rout of evanescence

Time stiff with thought hedges

Another glorified believer whips to

Linger by heart & then sign your name

Ladling of pulp unopened concocting

Transitive accident rockets begin

Angst but neutral scribble scribble slug

Riddled with false pretenses

Causally all by ourselves recoup

Lowing curiosity dislocations of privacy

Great shapes of the sentence

Indemnify fragment eager to disturb

Fair copy from the fact cake

Pang to attention repairs captivity

Graphic delirium in diction filler

[To] soothe shock doomed to

Insincerity startle longer

Lavender neck roulette in shorthand more pivotal

Patronizingly vow upon animal fit

As ardent too many gifts a bias

Daughterish vaulting in virtue

Intervals too dinky

All the heedlessness conjectured jelly little clutchings

Resist luscious noisy laughing stock as pillow

That there should be no particularization

Powder for filibuster contents

Fine reprove too confiding fervent

Dollar up new jewel bookcases of milk

Pawning suppose heads of poppies

Democracy wall: [the] general insecurity

Tumblers in the shade amid subdued suffrage

Hoovering their belongings into

Historical scale lap depasse

Fits the proper business of

Beast more timely choose only

Dormant pink cheek balked synopsis

Brute news is good news

Italics do not intercept allusion

Storms for contraceptives

Merit diffused

NOTE ON THE AUTHOR

NOTE ON THE AUTHOR

Bruce Andrews was born in Chicago on April Fools Day, 1948. He is the author of several dozen books of poetry and performance scores, most recently, *Lip Service* (Coach House Press, 2001). His essays on poetics are collected in *Paradise & Method: Poetics & Praxis* (Northwestern University Press, 1996). He was co-editor, with Charles Bernstein, of *L=A=N=G=U=A=G=E* (1978-1982) and *The L=A=N=G=U=A=G=E Book* (Southern Illinois University Press, 1984). Andrews has taught Political Science at Fordham University since 1975 — with a focus on global capitalism, U.S. imperialism, the politics of communication, conspiracy theory, and covert politics. In New York City, he has also been involved in a long series of collaborative multi-media theatrical projects and performances. As composer, sound designer & live mixer, since the mid 1980s, he has been Music Director for Sally Silvers & Dancers.

Also from Chax Press

Glen Mott, *Analects on a Chinese Screen*
Tim Peterson, *Since I Moved In*
Linda Russo, *Mirth*
Jefferson Carter, *Sentimental Blue*
Joe Amato, *Under Virga*
Charles Borkhuis, *After Image*
David Abel, *Black Valentine*
Paul Naylor, *Arranging Nature*
Kass Fleisher, *Accidental Species*
Tenney Nathanson, *Erased Art*
Heather Nagami, *Hostile*
Linh Dinh, *American Tatts*
Jonathan Brannen, *Deaccessioned Landscapes*
Beverly Dahlen, *A-Reading Spicer & 18 Sonnets*
Elizabeth Treadwell, *Chantry*
Allison Cobb, *Born Two*

For our many additional titles please visit
our web site: http://chax.org/

Chax Press is supported by the Tucson Pima Arts
Council and by the Arizona Commission on the Arts
with funding from the State of Arizona and the National
Endowment for the Arts.